LIMERICK POEMS

By Ruthie Van Oosbree ✦ Poems by Lauren Kukla

Big Buddy Books
An Imprint of Abdo Publishing
abdobooks.com

abdobooks.com

Published by Abdo Publishing, a division of ABDO, PO Box 398166, Minneapolis, Minnesota 55439.

Printed in the United States of America, North Mankato, Minnesota
052022
092022

Design: Emily O'Malley, Mighty Media, Inc.
Production: Mighty Media, Inc.
Editor: Jessica Rusick
Cover Photograph: FatCamera/iStockphoto
Interior Photographs: Bangkok Click Studio/Shutterstock Images, p. 29; Dashikka/Shutterstock Images, p. 7 (hen); drawkman/Shutterstock Images, p. 14; Early Spring/Shutterstock Images, p. 20; fizkes/Shutterstock Images, p. 23; Giuseppe Vitagliano/Shutterstock Images, p. 5; HappyPictures/Shutterstock Images, p. 7 (owl); irin-k/Shutterstock Images, p. 27 (insects); Jacek Chabraszewski/Shutterstock Images, p. 24; Kim Reinick/Shutterstock Images, p. 21; Lars Poyansky/Shutterstock Images, p. 7 (beard); LittleBee80/iStockphoto, p. 16; martinedoucet/iStockphoto, p. 11; New Africa/Shutterstock Images, p. 27 (cake); NotionPic/Shutterstock Images, p. 15 (both); Prostock-studio/Shutterstock Images, p. 13; Robert Kneschke/Shutterstock Images, p. 19; Rvector/Shutterstock Images, p. 17; Sam iSam Miller/Shutterstock Images, p. 27 (superhero); Sira Anamwong/Shutterstock Images, p. 25
Design Elements: mhatzapa/Shutterstock Images (paper doodles); Mighty Media, Inc. (backgrounds)

Library of Congress Control Number: 2021953303

Publisher's Cataloging-in-Publication Data
Names: Van Oosbree, Ruthie; Kukla, Lauren, authors.
Title: Limerick poems / by Ruthie Van Oosbree and Lauren Kukla
Description: Minneapolis, Minnesota : Abdo Publishing, 2023 | Series: Poetry power | Includes online resources and index.
Identifiers: ISBN 9781532198953 (lib. bdg.) | ISBN 9781098272883 (ebook)
Subjects: LCSH: Poetry--Juvenile literature. | Poetry and children--Juvenile literature. | Children's limericks--Juvenile literature. | Rhyme--Juvenile literature.
Classification: DDC 821.0--dc23

CONTENTS

LIMERICKS

A limerick is a type of poem. It has five lines. Limericks are usually funny and **nonsensical**.

Nursery **rhymes** have been written in limerick form for hundreds of years. The poems became popular in the late 1800s and early 1900s.

Some historians believe the limerick is named for the town or county of Limerick, Ireland.

English writer Edward Lear helped make limericks popular. Lear wrote a book of limericks called *A Book of* ***Nonsense***. It was published in 1846. One of Lear's famous poems is "There Was an Old Man with a Beard."

TIPS & TRICKS

How many nursery **rhymes** can you name that are limericks? One is "Hickory Dickory Dock."

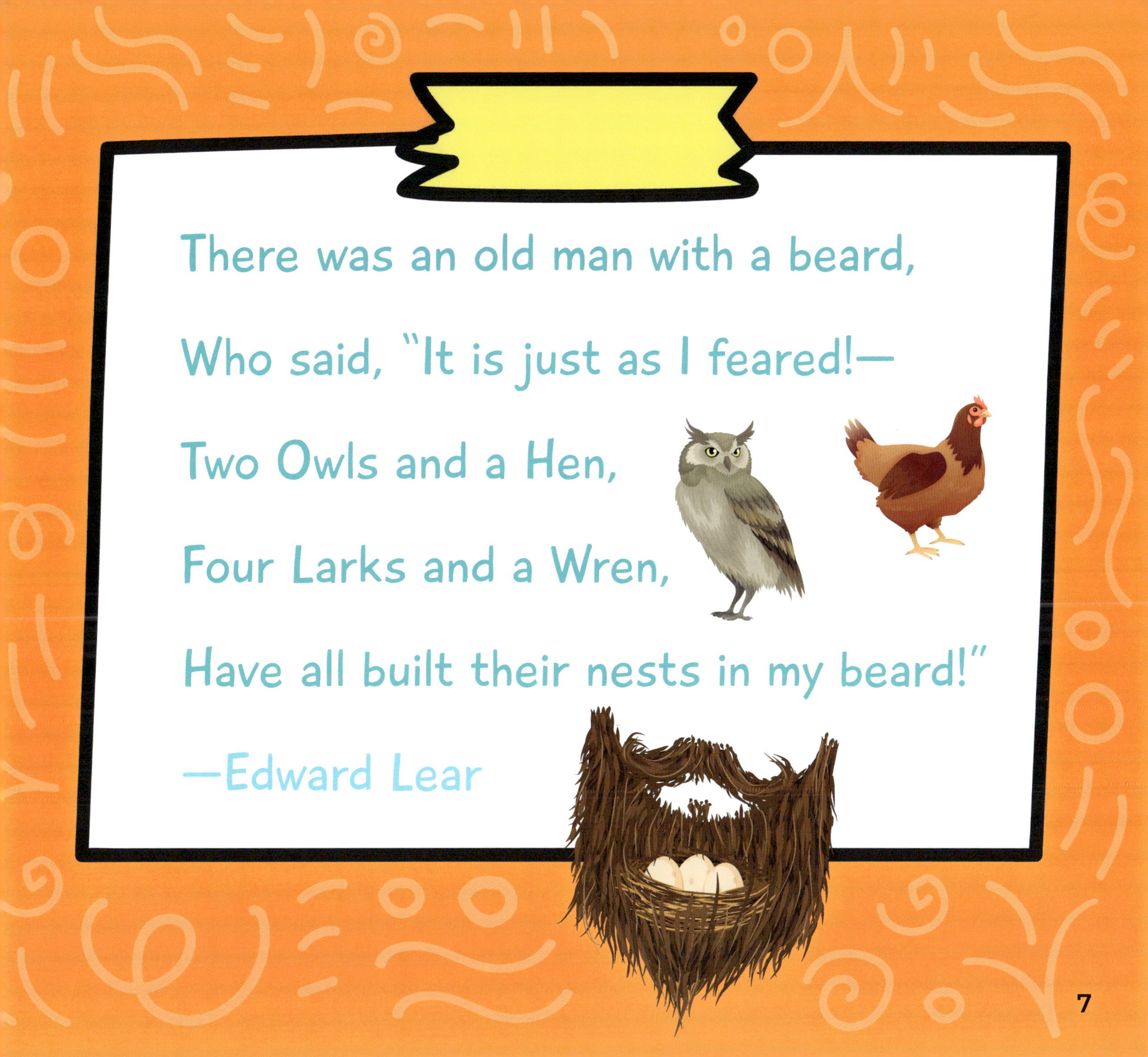

There was an old man with a beard,
Who said, "It is just as I feared!—
Two Owls and a Hen,
Four Larks and a Wren,
Have all built their nests in my beard!"

—Edward Lear

FITTING THE FORM

The first, second, and fifth lines of a limerick **rhyme**. The third and fourth lines also rhyme.

Limericks have a certain **meter**. Their lines are patterns of stressed and unstressed **syllables**. The stressed syllables are said with more **emphasis** than unstressed syllables.

LIMERICK METER

da DUM da da DUM da da DUM	There WAS an old MAN with a BEARD,
da DUM da da DUM da da DUM	Who SAID, "It is JUST as I FEARED!—
da DUM da da DUM	Two OWLS and a HEN,
da DUM da da DUM	Four LARKS and a WREN,
da DUM da da DUM da da DUM	Have ALL built their NESTS in my BEARD!"

da = unstressed syllable   DUM = stressed syllable

Limericks tell stories. There is often a main character introduced in the first line. The next lines describe the setting or action.

Often, the last line of a limerick is unexpected. It may reveal a surprise ending to the story!

TIPS & TRICKS

Many limericks start with the phrase "There once was a . . ." Try using this phrase in your limericks.

Read your limerick aloud to check its meter and rhymes.

ANIMAL LIMERICKS

Animals are great limerick subjects. They often do funny and unexpected things. Try writing a limerick about an animal doing something odd.

Start the poem by introducing the animal. Then describe where the animal is.

Your pet could be the main character in a limerick.

Next, describe what happens to the animal. Maybe the animal can speak or drive a car. The sillier, the better!

List words related to the animal or story. Find three words that **rhyme**. Then find two other words that rhyme. Write lines that end with these words.

A cow took a ride in a jeep
To visit her neighbor the sheep
The farmer just said,
"Oh, she's gone to bed—
I won't wake a sheep that's asleep."

GROSS LIMERICKS

Gross things can be funny topics for limericks. You might be inspired by something gross that happened to you. Or **brainstorm** things that gross you out, like slime or moldy food. Think of funny stories involving these objects.

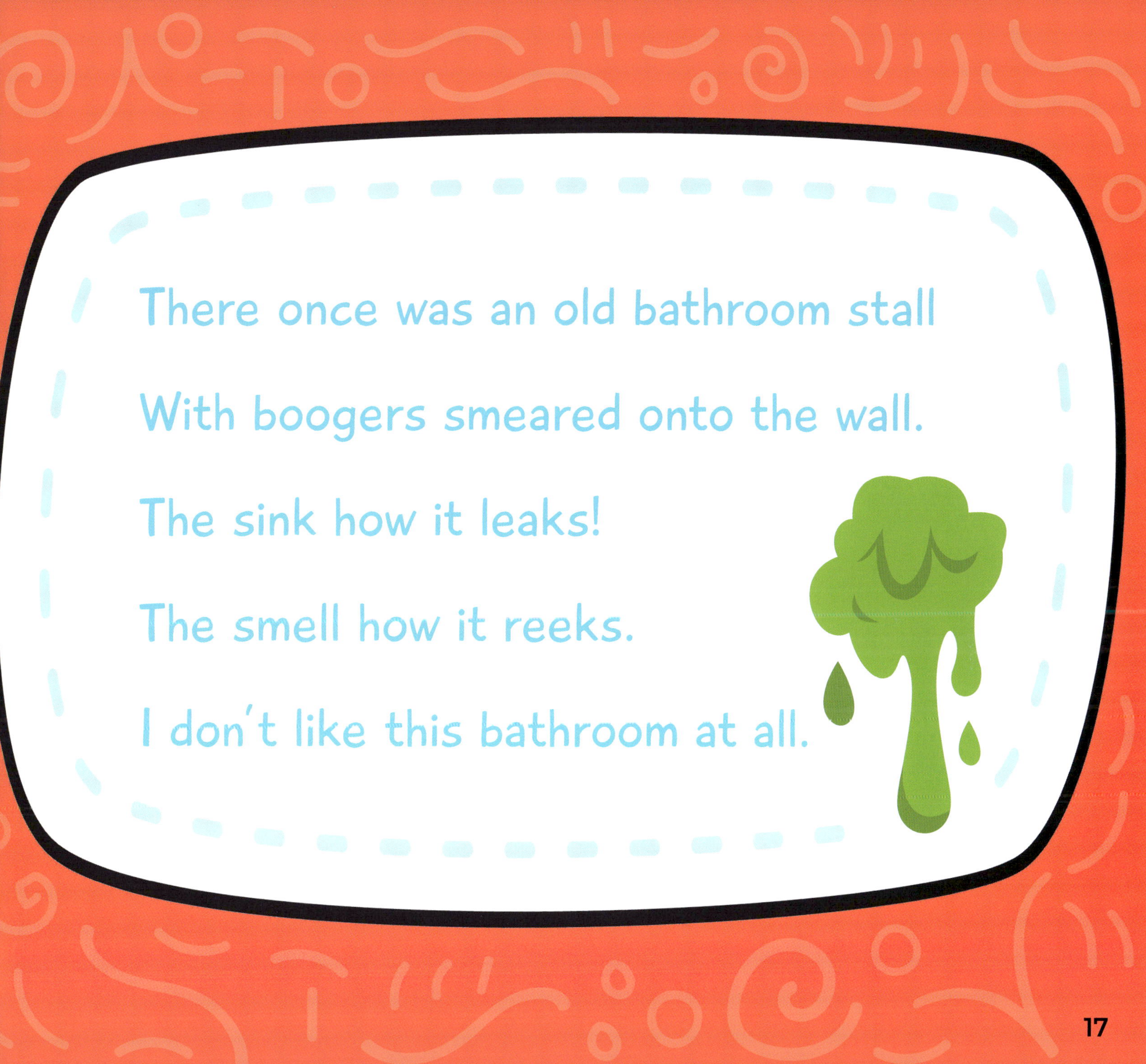

There once was an old bathroom stall
With boogers smeared onto the wall.
The sink how it leaks!
The smell how it reeks.
I don't like this bathroom at all.

SCHOOL LIMERICKS

School can also inspire your limericks. Write a limerick set in your classroom. It may be about something that really happened. Or it could be something you make up. Your poem doesn't have to be **realistic**!

Try writing about your favorite game to play at recess.

Think about the people at your school. This can include friends, teachers, and other staff. What are some unusual or surprising things they do? You could also write about your favorite school subject.

At school when you're waiting for lunch

And wish for some chow you could crunch

Just look to the floor

To find crumbs galore!

Not only one snack but a bunch.

FRIENDSHIP LIMERICKS

Try writing a friendship limerick. Write about something silly you and a friend do together. Or describe the way you met. Your friendship poem could also be about an imaginary situation you and a friend are in.

An imaginary friend or stuffed animal can be a great subject for a limerick.

Write down words that **rhyme** with your name and your friend's name. Also write down words that rhyme with your friend's favorite activities. Use these words to come up with ideas for the poem.

I have a best friend who's called Nate.

He likes to stay up very late.

He's playing Fortnite

In moonlight so bright.

He's tired when school starts at eight!

FAVORITE CHARACTER LIMERICKS

A limerick can also feature your favorite character. The character might be from a book or movie. It can also be made up! Point out something silly about the character. Or think of a goofy thing that could happen to them.

When Spider Guy wants something sweet

What snack does he whip up to eat?

Does he eat a cake

Or chocolate shake?

Or does he eat bugs for his treat?

SHARING YOUR LIMERICK

Limericks are fun to read aloud. They are also fun to listen to! Record yourself reading your poem aloud. Then share the recording. You can also write your limerick on paper. Then hang the poem up!

Draw a funny picture to go with your limerick.

GLOSSARY

brainstorm—to come up with a solution to a problem.

emphasis—added force given when speaking.

meter—the structure of the number of syllables and places of emphasis in lines of poetry.

nonsensical—not making sense or having any meaning. Nonsensical words, ideas, or behaviors are nonsense.

realistic—showing something that could happen in real life.

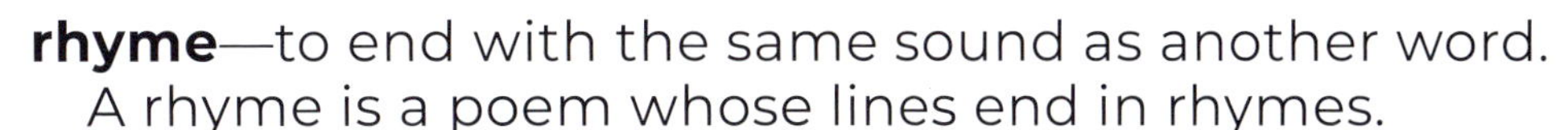

rhyme—to end with the same sound as another word. A rhyme is a poem whose lines end in rhymes.

syllable—one of the parts a word is divided into based on the way it is pronounced. A syllable usually contains one vowel sound.

ONLINE RESOURCES

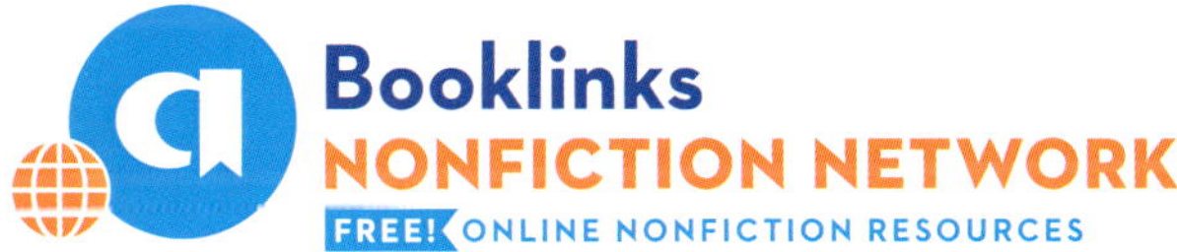

To learn more about limerick poems, please visit **abdobooklinks.com** or scan this QR code. These links are routinely monitored and updated to provide the most current information available.

INDEX